The Millionaire Mindset

How to Overcome the Hurdles and Succeed in Business

By

Lonnie Wilcher

Table of Contents

Introduction

Chapter One: The Beginning

The Influence of Belief and Imagery

The Art of Growth Mindset

Chapter Two: Getting Past Mental Obstacles

How to Recognize and Get Rid of Limiting Beliefs

Cultivating a Positive Attitude

Fear and Risk Management

Chapter Three: Excellent Work Ethic

Discipline and Persistence

Improving Your Time Management Skills

Do Not Stop Learning

Chapter Four: The Development of Financial Intelligence

Money and Wealth

Making a Strategic Financial Plan

Developing Your Investing Art

Chapter Five: The Influence of Connections

Effective Relationship Building and Communication

Role Models and Mentors

Chapter Six: Overcoming Challenges and Rebounding

Resilience and the Art of Bouncing Back

Failure into Opportunities

Chapter Seven: The Millionaire Mindset in Action

Stories of Entrepreneurial Success

Conclusion

Introduction

Business success is not exclusively based on outside variables like industry trends or market conditions. A person's thinking frequently distinguishes them from others and drives them toward greatness. The Millionaire Mindset is a potent force that helps people to overcome obstacles and achieve amazing success in the realm of entrepreneurship and wealth creation.

This book, "The Millionaire Mindset: How to Overcome the Hurdles and Succeed in Business," discusses the fundamental ideas, methods, and attitudes that makeup billionaires' mindsets. This book is a thorough tool for unlocking your potential and embracing the mentality that will lead you to financial prosperity and fulfillment. It draws on years of research, actual experiences, and insights from great entrepreneurs.

Let me share with you my personal story before we start this revolutionary adventure. Like a lot of individuals, I started out in poverty. I personally experienced the hardships and restrictions that frequently go along with a lack of financial resources growing up in a small town. When I was younger, my family and I had ongoing financial difficulties, and I yearned for a better life.

I set out on a mission to uncover the success secrets because I was determined to escape the cycle of shortage. I read voraciously, went to seminars, and looked for mentors who could show me the way to success. Years of trial and error led me to the gradual realization that one's thinking is the key to success and prosperity.

I came to understand that millionaires and prosperous businesspeople had a certain way of thinking, a mindset that allowed them to perceive possibilities where others saw hurdles, to take calculated risks, and to persevere in the face of difficulty. This epiphany marked a turning point in my life, and I made a commitment to comprehending and adopting the mindset of these extraordinarily successful people.

I saw a dramatic transformation as I implemented the Millionaire Mindset's ideas in my own life and business pursuits. Where I had previously perceived obstacles, I started to see opportunity. I was able to overcome obstacles with grace and tenacity because I had a robust spirit, amazing right? Most significantly, I learned that the actual measure of success is not only how wealthy we are, but also how much of an impact we have on others' lives and how much of a legacy we leave behind.

My goal in writing this book is to impart the priceless lessons and methods I discovered while embracing the Millionaire Mindset. This book will provide you with the skills and mentality needed to overcome obstacles and achieve amazing success in your company and in life, whether you're a fledgling entrepreneur, an aspiring business leader, or someone looking to improve their financial situation.

This book's chapters will explore various facets of the millionaire mindset while offering helpful tips, doable ideas, and motivational tales to help you adopt and live by these ideas. We will examine the fundamental components that characterize the mindset of billionaires, from comprehending and overcoming mental obstacles to defining precise goals, developing a strong work ethic, and acquiring financial acumen.

We'll also discuss the value of mindfulness and visualization, the value of forming solid connections and networks, and the skill of recovering from failures. You will learn more about the mindset needed to successfully navigate the complicated world of business and entrepreneurship through each chapter and how to apply these ideas to your own life.

It's important to keep in mind that anyone who is willing to go on the path can nurture and develop the millionaire mindset. It is my genuine wish that this book will act as a road map for you, enabling you to overcome challenges, realize your full potential, and start along a path to material prosperity and personal fulfillment.

Are you prepared to adopt the Millionaire Mindset and revamp your existence? Join me as we set out on this amazing tour.

Chapter One

The Beginning

You've probably heard someone mention the millionaire attitude if you pay any attention to social media or follow any influencers. It's ingrained in the hustler culture. What exactly does it imply when someone mentions having a millionaire mindset or that you need one? Does everyone learn it on their own?

It's not about earning a million dollars that defines a millionaire mindset. It's not even about your bank account, real estate, financial security, or living in a penthouse in New York.

According to individuals who swear by it, having a millionaire mindset entails concentrating on altering your life, beginning with your perspective, in order to achieve the objectives you've always wished to realize. It's also not a simple task. Every day, you must promote intentional behaviors and ways of thinking.

According to the theory, millionaires reside in an environment of wealth that enables them to achieve more achievement and self-assurance. You must first act as though you have already accomplished your goals if you wish to succeed. Your success there fuels additional success.

A millionaire attitude does not emerge overnight. It requires vision, fervor, and a tremendous amount of effort. Recognize that any setbacks are typical and serve as a learning opportunity. Have patience and awareness. Confidence and financial freedom are easily attainable if you are clear about your objectives and stay motivated.

The Influence of Belief and Imagery

Belief is a potent force that molds our reality by influencing our thoughts, deeds, and behaviors. It serves as the framework for the Millionaire Mindset. The boundaries or opportunities we perceive in our life depend on our ideas about who we are, what we are capable of, and our potential determine the limits or possibilities we see in our lives. We may unlock our entire potential and achieve remarkable achievements by utilizing the power of believing.

The first step in believing is having the conviction that we are capable of greatness and that our goals and desires are attainable. Our ability to overcome self-doubt, endure difficulties, and maintain focus on our objectives is a result of deep-seated confidence. We radiate confidence and draw opportunities that support our beliefs when we genuinely trust in our abilities and selves.

What Visualization Can Do

Visualization is a potent tool that strengthens and magnifies the effects of believing. It entails visualizing our intended outcomes clearly in our minds and feeling them as if they have already been realized. When we visualize, we use our senses and emotions to communicate with our subconscious mind exactly what we want to manifest in our life.

We unleash the creative potential of our minds when we vividly picture our objectives. Because our subconscious mind cannot distinguish between genuine experiences and imagined ones, visualizing our desired outcomes in great detail helps us program our thoughts for success. It increases our sense of possibility and harmonizes our ideas, feelings, and deeds with our objectives.

I was on a job that wasn't rewarding and didn't match my genuine hobbies and objectives a few years ago. I had a deep-seated understanding that I was capable of doing more and building an abundant life, but self-doubt and limiting beliefs prevented me from doing so.

During this time, I learned about the Millionaire Mindset, the power of believing, and the power of visualizing. I made the decision to fully dedicate myself to studying and using these principles because I was intrigued by the potential. I began by developing a solid belief in my own ability and skills. I overcame my negative ideas and restricting beliefs that had kept me from moving forward for so long, and I substituted empowering beliefs for them.

I confirmed optimistic phrases about my skills, my deservingness of achievement, and my limitless potential through daily affirmations. I vividly pictured the success, abundance, and fulfillment I wanted for my ideal life. I envisioned myself as a prosperous businessperson who was financially independent and made a difference in the lives of others.

I observed a striking change in my mentality and my actions as I kept up my belief and visualization practices. I developed more self-assurance, clarity, and initiative. Even in the face of difficulties, I persisted in moving in the direction of my objectives. Doors started to open, chances started to present themselves, and I started to draw in individuals and resources that would help me on my quest.

My compass turned into belief and imagery, which fueled my willpower and helped me move forward. I turned my passion into a successful business that exceeded all of my expectations. In addition to assisting me in achieving financial success, the power of belief and visualization also gave my life meaning and fulfillment.

Through my own path, I've discovered that visualization and belief are effective means of bringing about the desires we have. The world works in our favor to make our objectives a reality when we genuinely believe in ourselves and our aspirations and when we imagine them with unshakable focus and passion. The gasoline that fires our potential and drives us toward success is belief and imagery.

The chapters that follow will examine realistic methods and tactics for developing faith and improving visualization abilities so that you can use them to overcome obstacles and experience extraordinary success in both business and life. Keep in mind that your thoughts determine your reality, and visualization is the link that makes it possible for your desires to come true. Accept the power of visualization and belief, and watch as your life changes right before your very eyes.

The Art of Growth Mindset

The idea of a growth mindset, made popular by psychologist Carol Dweck, is a game-changing strategy for both professional and personal advancement. It is a way of thinking that supports the notion that we may improve our skills and intelligence by working hard, making an effort, and never stopping to study. A fixed mindset, on the other hand, is the idea that our characteristics and skills are unchangeable, fixed traits.

The growth mentality understands that obstacles, failures, and setbacks all present chances for development and learning. It inspires people to welcome the path of growth, view challenges as stepping stones to achievement, and persevere in the face of difficulty. We may reach our maximum potential and produce remarkable achievements by developing a growth mindset.

Gains from a Growth Mindset

Numerous advantages of a development mindset enable people to overcome challenges and achieve extraordinary achievements, including:

Resilience and Perseverance: People with a growth mindset are aware that failures and setbacks are a necessary part of learning. They see difficulties as chances to learn and become more resilient. When someone has a development mentality, setbacks don't define them; instead, they serve as important lessons that help them move forward. They continue to work for their objectives after failing but with renewed vigor.

Embracing Learning and Growth: A growth mindset encourages a love of learning as well as a desire to investigate novel concepts and opportunities. People that adopt this approach actively look for chances to increase their knowledge and skill sets. They welcome criticism and view it as an important tool for development. Continuous learning becomes a way of life for them, allowing them to adapt and succeed in a constantly changing environment.

Increased work and Motivation: A growth mindset encourages individuals to put up the extra work necessary to achieve success. This type of person is aware that effort and hard work are necessary for development and success. They are prepared to put in the time and effort necessary to hone their abilities, perfect their trade, and strive for excellence. Their inspiration comes from the satisfaction of making progress and the delight of learning.

Agility and adaptability: People with a growth mindset can accept change and adjust their behavior in response to it. They are not constrained or limited in their ideas. Instead, they take a flexible and creative approach to problems, looking for novel solutions. They can deal with uncertainty thanks to their versatility, and they do well in changing circumstances.

Increased Self-confidence: Self-confidence is cultivated by the growth mindset, which results in an increase in self-assurance. This way of thinking is shared by those who are confident in their capacity to learn, develop, and conquer obstacles. They view obstacles as passing phases and blame ignorance or ineffectiveness for them rather than inborn restrictions. They advance because of this self-assurance, which empowers them to take chances and seize possibilities.

How to Develop a Growth Mindset

A growth mentality involves deliberate effort and dedication to one's own development. Stated below are some tools for developing a growth mindset:

Embrace Difficulties: Rather than avoiding difficulties, look for them as chances for improvement. Push your boundaries by engaging in new events outside of your comfort zone. Embrace difficulties with a positive outlook and the knowledge that they are stepping stones to advancement.

Put an emphasis on the effort and the process rather than just the results. Honor the work you put into your projects and appreciate the importance of perseverance. Accept the process of development and progress while keeping in mind that success comes from persistent effort.

Consider Failures as Learning Opportunities: Reframe failures and setbacks as beneficial learning opportunities. Draw lessons from these encounters and use them to improve your strategy. Recognize setbacks as brief setbacks that are a normal part of the growing process.

Develop a Passion for Learning: Become passionate about learning and actively seek out opportunities to learn new things. Read books, enroll in classes, go to workshops, and do things that expand and test your abilities. Adopt the philosophy of lifelong learning.

Foster a Positive and Supportive Environment: Create a positive and encouraging environment by surrounding oneself with others who value development. Find peers that share your values and are growth-minded as mentors, coaches, and coaches. Participate in discussions that further education, teamwork, and personal growth.

Practice Self-Reflection: Reflect on your attitudes, beliefs, and behaviors on a regular basis. Replace any fixed mentality thinking with perspectives that are growth-oriented. Recognize your self-limiting beliefs and seek to replace them with powerful ones.

Remember that by developing a development mentality, you can access a world of opportunities and create the way for extraordinary success. Accept challenges, keep going despite setbacks, and make a commitment to ongoing learning and development. There are no restrictions on your potential when you adopt a development mentality.

Chapter Two

Getting Past Mental Obstacles

Our self-limiting ideas are what are known as mental barriers. These ideas have the potential to hold us back from acting or making progress if we let them. You might be prevented from producing that book, accepting that promotion, or pursuing that relationship by a mental barrier, for instance.

Even when you desire to undertake these things, focusing too much on limiting beliefs may cause you to believe that you lack the skills or abilities necessary to pursue them.

Mental barriers, also known as emotional or psychological barriers, might appear in our ideas, feelings, or behavior toward others. They frequently act out of dread, for instance:

- Anxiety of failing

- Anxiety about the future

- Anxiety of falling short

They can influence not just your actions (or lack thereof), but also your capacity to engage or communicate with others, or even with yourself.

Most people encounter mental obstacles at some point in their lives. While some people can readily overcome mental challenges, others can find it more challenging.

How to Recognize and Get Rid of Limiting Beliefs

Deeply rooted attitudes and beliefs known as "limiting beliefs" limit our potential and prevent us from reaching our objectives. Through our experiences, interactions, and societal indoctrination, these beliefs are frequently developed early in life. They set restrictions on ourselves, influencing how we view our capabilities.

Limiting beliefs can have an impact on a variety of areas of our lives, such as our work, relationships, and personal growth. They may damage our self-esteem, discourage us from taking chances, and impede our advancement. However, we can overcome these limitations and realize our full potential by recognizing and contesting these ideas.

The Repercussion of Limiting Beliefs

I had a strong urge to launch my own business many years ago. But I struggled with self-doubt and a firm conviction that success belonged to others, not to me. I had self-sabotaging thoughts like "I'm not good enough," "I don't have what it takes," and "I'm destined to struggle financially."

These ideas developed into substantial roadblocks in my development. They prevented me from acting, looking for chances, and completely dedicating myself to my entrepreneurial goals. My anxieties and limiting beliefs left me mired in a cycle of self-defeat, where they held me captive to passivity and mediocrity.

I came to a turning point one day. I came to the realization that these ideas did not serve me and prevented me from leading a fulfilling life. No matter how deeply ingrained they were, I pledged to recognize and dispel my limiting ideas. I was able to escape the trap that way.

Knowing Your Limiting Beliefs

Being aware of limiting beliefs is the first step towards getting rid of them. The following techniques will assist you in recognizing your own limiting beliefs:

Self-Reflection:

Spend some time reflecting on yourself and your life. Find out whether any of your beliefs are preventing you from realizing your greatest potential. Pay attention to negative patterns and repeating thoughts that appear in various aspects of your life.

Journaling:

Keep a notebook to track your ideas, feelings, and inner dialogue. If any limiting or negative beliefs come to mind, write them down.

Investigate the reasons behind these ideas and how they affect your outlook and behavior.

Requesting comments:

Contact dependable friends, coaches, or mentors who can offer unbiased opinions and criticism. They might assist you in identifying limiting ideas and blind spots that you might not be aware of.

Speculative Presumptions:

Consider whether your beliefs are true. Are they supported by actual data or just conjecture? Look for facts to refute your limiting assumptions and take into account alternate viewpoints.

Beating Limiting Beliefs

Please keep in mind that changing limiting beliefs is a process that takes time, persistence, and self-compassion. Here are some ways for challenging and overcoming limiting beliefs:

(1) Reframing: Replace your limiting thoughts with powerful and positive beliefs. Check this for instance, instead of thinking "I'm not good enough," reframe it to be "I can succeed and grow in any area I venture into."

(2) Affirmations: To offset negative self-talk, use positive affirmations. Repeat empowering statements that both challenge and

reinforce new, good attitudes. Say to yourself, "I am deserving of success and capable of achieving my goals."

(3)   Visualization: Use visualization to build mental images of yourself successfully overcoming obstacles and reaching your goals. Imagine yourself confidently moving out of your comfort zone and seizing fresh chances.

(4)   Acting: Break the pattern of passivity by taking little moves toward your objectives. Every single step forward promotes the conviction that you are capable of development. Celebrate your accomplishments and use them to demonstrate your ability.

(5)   Personal Development and Continuous Learning: Invest in your personal growth and development. Learn new things, practice new talents, and surround yourself with people that inspire and support your growth. Participating in personal development activities boosts confidence and encourages belief in one's own abilities.

Accepting a New Narrative

My Personal Transformation

I gradually overcome my limiting notions via constant effort and self-reflection. I called my negative self-talk into question and reframed my views to be more empowering and supportive. I became engrossed in personal growth, seeking mentors, taking workshops, and reading books that inspired and empowered me.

My confidence developed when I began to take action and venture outside of my comfort zone. I recognized that my restricting beliefs were just illusions that were preventing me from achieving the success I was capable of. I launched my own business, endured hurdles, and persevered in the face of disappointments.

My new beliefs gradually supplanted my old, restricting ones. I accepted a new story, one that gave me the confidence to take risks, embrace progress, and live a life of richness and fulfillment. Not only in my work but also in my personal life, the revolution was deep. As I smashed the self-imposed constraints that had held me back for so long, I felt a sense of liberty and exhilaration.

Identifying and overcoming limiting beliefs is a lifelong journey of self-discovery and development. We open ourselves up to new possibilities and release our actual potential by challenging our beliefs and replacing them with inspiring narratives. Remember that you have the ability to rewrite your tale and live a life of boundless possibility and achievement.

Cultivating a Positive Attitude

A positive attitude is a state of mind that influences our ideas, feelings, and behaviors, resulting in a more fulfilling and successful existence. It is the ability to face life's challenges with optimism, resilience, and self-confidence. Cultivating a good attitude benefits not only our own well-being but also the connections we form and the goals we aspire to achieve. We may transform adversity into opportunity, overcome setbacks with grace, and inspire people around us by adopting a positive attitude.

The ability to reframe our thoughts and perceptions is a vital element of cultivating a good attitude. It is about making a conscious decision to focus on the positive parts of any scenario rather than the negative. This does not imply ignoring or rejecting difficulties, but rather tackling them with a solution-oriented mindset. We can find lessons and opportunities for progress in even the most challenging circumstances by reframing our thoughts.

A positive attitude also entails learning to be resilient in the face of setbacks and failures. It is about accepting that setbacks are a natural part of life and utilizing them to propel oneself forward. Failures can be viewed as chances for learning and progress rather than as permanent or personal reflections of our worth. A positive attitude enables us to recover from setbacks with renewed motivation and the conviction that success is within our grasp.

Developing a positive mindset necessitates self-compassion and self-care. It is about physically, emotionally, and mentally caring for ourselves. Taking care of our physical health through exercise, the right nutrition, and adequate rest aids in the maintenance of a cheerful attitude. Similarly, doing things that make us happy, practicing gratitude, and surrounding ourselves with positive influences all contribute to having a positive attitude in life.

The power of positive self-talk is another important part of cultivating a good attitude. Our inner conversation has a significant impact on our attitudes and views. We may enhance our self-confidence and strengthen our positive thinking by replacing negative self-talk with affirming and encouraging words. Positive self-talk assists us in overcoming self-doubt, overcoming obstacles, and embracing new opportunities.

Developing a happy attitude also entails deliberately choosing our reactions and responses to external situations. Remember, every scenario might not be controlled but we can change how we perceive and react to them. We may develop positive connections and create a helpful and harmonious environment by responding with compassion, understanding, and empathy. Our optimistic attitude can spread and inspire and uplift people around us.

It is critical to understand that having a happy attitude does not imply ignoring life's truths or suppressing bad feelings. It is about intentionally choosing to focus on the good features and prospects while identifying and processing negative feelings. It is a delicate balance of accepting the entire range of human emotions while actively building a positive outlook.

In my own life, cultivating a happy mindset has had a transforming effect. There were times when I experienced substantial hurdles and failures that put my determination to the test. I was able to locate strength and perseverance within myself by actively adopting a good mindset. I reframed challenges as chances for growth, focused on solutions rather than issues, and maintained my optimism in the face of hardship. This cheerful attitude not only helped me overcome obstacles but also inspired and uplifted everyone around me.

Fear and Risk Management

Fear and risk are inextricably linked in life. They are connected to our lives, decisions, and dreams. Fear, which is often motivated by uncertainty and the likelihood of undesirable outcomes, can paralyze us and prevent us from taking essential risks. However, controlling fear and risk is critical for personal development, success, and living a meaningful life. We can break free from the limits of fear, accept measured risks, and realize our entire potential by recognizing and negotiating these factors.

Fear is a natural human reaction designed to keep us safe from perceived threats. It is a natural reaction that causes a variety of emotions such as fear, doubt, and apprehension. While fear can be beneficial in some situations, such as avoiding physical danger, it can also limit our potential when it becomes excessive and unreasonable.

Understanding the underlying causes of fear and identifying the ways in which it may be holding us back are the first steps in managing it. Fear is frequently motivated by apprehension about failure, rejection, or the unknown. It may be based on previous experiences, cultural expectations, or self-imposed constraints. We can face our worries directly and dispute their validity by pinpointing the source of our fears.

Reframing our perspective is an excellent fear-management method. We can choose to see fear as an opportunity for progress and self-discovery rather than as a negative force. Fear can act as a compass, directing our attention to areas that require it and providing useful insights into our ambitions and objectives. We can acquire the resilience and fortitude needed to move forward by reframing fear as a normal part of the journey.

Another important part of dealing with fear is developing self-compassion and practicing self-care. Fear can drain you emotionally, generating tension and anxiety. We can nourish our well-being and increase emotional resilience by prioritizing self-care activities such as exercise, meditation, and hobbies. Taking care of ourselves allows us to approach fear with confidence and stability.

Risk, on the other hand, is an unavoidable component of growth and achievement. Taking chances entails moving outside of our comfort zones and into the unknown. It necessitates embracing ambiguity and accepting the risk of failure. While dangers might be frightening, they also provide chances for growth, learning, and reaching our objectives.

Risk management is striking a balance between reasoned decision-making and seizing chances. It is about evaluating probable outcomes, calculating potential rewards against potential losses, and making educated decisions. Calculated risks necessitate extensive investigation, analysis, and assessment of our available resources, talents, and assistance. We may reduce potential negative repercussions and boost our chances of success by identifying the risks involved and preparing contingency measures.

It is critical to create a growth mentality in order to effectively manage risk. Failures and setbacks can be viewed as learning experiences and stepping stones toward success when we have a growth attitude. It allows us to accept challenges and persevere in the face of hardship. We regard risks as chances for personal and professional development when we have a growth mindset, knowing that even if the outcome is not as planned, we can learn and grow from the experience.

Building a support system is also essential in dealing with fear and risk. Surrounding ourselves with people who believe in us, guide us, and support us can boost our confidence and help us through difficult situations. Seeking mentor advice or networking with like-minded people can bring significant insights and views, making it simpler to control fear and take cautious risks.

In my own travels, I've come across several instances where fear and danger collided. I've struggled with self-doubt, uncertainty, and failure dread. However, by actively managing my anxiety and taking measured chances, I've been able to reach personal and professional milestones. It has necessitated stepping outside of my comfort zone, confronting my concerns head-on, and taking brave action. Every risk I've taken has yielded great lessons, personal growth, and unexpected benefits.

Chapter Three

Excellent Work Ethic

Have you ever pondered how to act professionally at work? It can be difficult to determine what behaviors and attitudes are and are not appropriate in various professional contexts during your career, especially in the early years. The more organizations and industries you visit, the clearer your understanding will become. When you're just starting out, it can be difficult to identify these tendencies.

Nonetheless, businesses are now expecting more from entry-level employees. Degrees from reputable institutions are insufficient. According to a 2022 Job Outlook poll, 87% of employers believe professionalism is highly important, yet just 44% of new graduates are adept at it. Companies and recruiting managers want to see your drive, positive attitude, and passion or dedication. To put it another way, they want to see that you have a strong work ethic.

As a young professional, this is critical to your long-term success. So, how can you establish a solid work ethic more quickly?

A strong work ethic is a basic trait that distinguishes individuals in their quest for success and achievement. It is a way of thinking and a set of values that shape one's approach to work, embracing dedication, discipline, responsibility, and a desire for perfection. Developing and maintaining a strong work ethic is critical for personal and professional development since it influences not just the quality of our work but also our reputation, opportunities, and overall success.

Discipline and Perseverance

Discipline and perseverance are two powerful traits that play an important part in obtaining success and reaching our objectives. They are vital characteristics that enable people to overcome challenges, stay focused on their goals, and persevere in the face of adversity. While talent and intelligence are important, discipline and tenacity are typically the deciding factors between those who achieve their goals and those who fall short. Let us investigate the significant impact of discipline and determination on personal and professional achievement.

Discipline: The key to maintaining consistency and focus.

Discipline is defined as the ability to manage one's behavior, ideas, and actions in order to achieve long-term goals. It entails making deliberate choices and following self-imposed norms and procedures. Individuals who practice discipline are able to maintain constancy in their efforts even when confronted with distractions, temptations, or challenges.

Creating Effective Habits

Discipline is about developing effective habits that promote personal and professional development. It entails establishing priorities, setting goals, and developing routines that support those goals. We can minimize the need for constant inspiration by building habits that support our goals and rely on discipline to propel us ahead regularly.

Postponing Gratification

Discipline frequently necessitates deferring current enjoyment in favor of long-term rewards. It entails avoiding the desire to engage in temporary pleasures or distractions that may impede progress. Individuals who practice discipline can make decisions that favor long-term goals over short-term pleasure.

Staying Focus and Concentrated

I will tell you that discipline is highly crucial for remaining focus and concentrated. In an age of endless distractions, maintaining discipline allows people to focus their attention and energy on meaningful work and goals. It enables people to ignore distractions, successfully manage their time, and remain engaged in tasks that contribute to their success.

Persistence: Overcoming Obstacles and Adversity

Persistence is defined as an unrelenting desire to pursue goals in the face of setbacks, failures, or problems. It measures how we cope in the face of adversity. Persistence enables people to see barriers as chances for progress and to learn from setbacks rather than give up.

Resilience in the Face of Failure

Persistence entails overcoming setbacks and using them as stepping stones to achievement. It is the ability to learn from mistakes, make adjustments, and keep moving forward. Individuals who cultivate persistence build resilience, which allows them to keep a good attitude and a feeling of purpose even when faced with challenges.

Getting Rid of Procrastination

Persistence is essential in overcoming procrastination and the desire to put off vital activities. It entails acting consistently and avoiding complacency. Individuals minimize the impact of procrastination and enhance their productivity by constantly working toward goals.

Accepting the Growth Mindset

Persistence is closely related to a growth mindset, which is the concept that abilities can be developed through hard work and practice. Individuals with a growth mentality see problems as chances to learn and progress, which fuels their perseverance. They recognize that success frequently necessitates perseverance and that setbacks are but temporary obstacles on the route to triumph.

Discipline and Persistence Have a Mutually Beneficial Relationship

Discipline and perseverance are inextricably linked and strengthen each other. Discipline provides the structure and consistency required to persevere in the face of adversity, whereas perseverance is dependent on discipline to sustain focus and commitment.

Individuals can build routines and habits that support their goals through discipline, while persistence ensures that those habits are maintained over time. Discipline lays the groundwork for perseverance by fostering the work ethic and self-control required to continue the course.

Similarly, persistence strengthens one's desire to stick to established routines and habits. Individuals who persevere in their efforts strengthen their discipline and generate a positive feedback loop, propelling them ahead.

In practice, discipline and perseverance go hand in hand to propel progress and achievement. Discipline offers structure and guidelines, whereas perseverance provides the determination and tenacity needed to overcome challenges along the path. They form a potent mix that enables people to stay focused, sustain momentum, and finally achieve their goals.

Improving Your Time Management Skills

Time is a valuable and limited resource that, when used well, can be a catalyst for personal and professional success. Developing good time management skills is a life-changing experience that allows people to prioritize activities, enhance productivity, and create a healthy work-life balance. Let me share with you how I began this adventure and saw the significant influence it made on my life.

I used to be overburdened and constantly battling to keep up with my commitments. I was balancing hard work, personal commitments, and furthering my education. I felt like there were never enough hours in the day to get everything done. This resulted in tension, exhaustion, and frustration as I saw vital things fall through the cracks.

Recognizing that I needed to make a difference, I set out on a journey to improve my time management abilities. Here are a few of the methods I used along the way:

✓ **Setting precise Goals:** I started by setting precise goals for both my personal and professional lives. I was able to better prioritize my work and manage time by having a clear vision of what I wanted to achieve. This clarity provided me with a sense of direction and purpose, allowing me to concentrate on what was genuinely important.

✓ **Prioritizing chores:** I learned the skill of prioritization as well as the significance of differentiating between urgent and significant chores. I prioritized the tasks that were most closely related to my objectives. This enabled me to make progress on major projects while also managing daily responsibilities.

✓ **Planning and organization:** To optimize my workflow, I used excellent planning and organization approaches. I began making daily, weekly, and monthly plans to organize my tasks and deadlines. Breaking down huge projects into smaller, manageable pieces enabled me to approach them in a more organized and systematic manner.

✓ **Time Blocking:** In my time management quest, time blocking was a game changer. I set aside time for various tasks such as concentrated work, meetings, breaks, and personal time. This strategy enabled me to remove distractions and focus during concentrated work periods.

✓ **Overcoming Procrastination:** Procrastination had been a huge impediment to good time management for me. I overcame this obstacle by splitting work down into smaller, more manageable chunks. I overcome the desire to postpone by taking tiny actions and focusing on incremental improvement.

✓ **Setting Boundaries and Learning to Say No:** I understood the need of setting boundaries and learning to say no to tasks or commitments that did not connect with my goals or overburdened my schedule. I generated space for activities that genuinely mattered and maintained a healthier work-life balance by valuing my time and emphasizing self-care.

I went through considerable changes during my time management journey. My productivity increased noticeably as I became more structured and focused on my priorities. I was able to accomplish more in less time by successfully organizing my time, giving me a higher sense of accomplishment and joy.

Furthermore, I noticed a decrease in tension and an improvement in my overall well-being. I felt more in control of my time and more peaceful and confident in managing my duties since I had a clear strategy and framework.

Developing good time management skills also enabled me to achieve a more harmonious work-life balance. I learned to set aside time for personal interests, hobbies, and self-care. This allowed me to relax and refresh, giving me the energy and determination to perform at my best.

One of the most notable benefits of learning efficient time management techniques was an improvement in my decision-making abilities. I became more strategic in my resource allocation and task prioritization. I learned to analyze opportunities and make educated decisions, ensuring that my time and energy were spent on activities that were in line with my aims and values.

Do Not Stop Learning

Building a passion for lifelong learning is essential for both personal and professional development in a world that is changing quickly. Beyond formal education, the pursuit of knowledge and skills is a lifetime adventure that equips people to adapt, invent, and succeed in a constantly shifting environment. People can reach their greatest potential, widen their horizons, and remain at the forefront of their areas by cultivating a real love of learning. Let's go into the importance of fostering a love of lifelong learning and look at ways to support this mindset.

The Value of Constant Learning

Understanding Change

Individuals are given the skills they need to adapt to change through continuous learning. Industries, technology, and trends evolve quickly in today's dynamic environment. Individuals that embrace a passion for learning keep ahead of the curve, embracing new concepts and methods, and remaining pertinent in their specialized industries.

Increasing Knowledge and Abilities

Individuals can increase their knowledge and skills by engaging in continuous learning. It provides chances to broaden one's knowledge, stay current on advances, and gain fresh perspectives. People can increase their understanding and creativity in problem-solving by actively seeking out new knowledge and experiences.

Promoting Creativity and Innovation

Innovation and creativity are fueled by a passion for lifelong learning. Individuals are better able to think critically, connect seemingly unrelated ideas, and come up with novel solutions when they are exposed to a variety of ideas and viewpoints. Breakthrough concepts and transformative thoughts thrive in an open, curious mind.

Individual and Professional Development

Growth in both the personal and professional spheres is sped up by continuous learning. It broadens networks, improves professional prospects, and opens doors to new possibilities. People who value lifelong learning are more flexible, resilient, and better able to deal with the challenges of contemporary life.

How to Develop a Passion for Lifelong Learning

At first, I was only concerned with formal education and thought that learning ended after I finished college. I soon became aware, though, of this mindset's limitations. I started my journey toward embracing continuous learning by implementing the aforementioned tactics.

I started making learning objectives, choosing my interests, and pursuing self-directed learning. I experimented with a variety of learning strategies and tools, including books, online courses, and podcasts. I actively looked for mentors and had conversations with like-minded people to broaden my knowledge and viewpoints.

I ingrained learning into my everyday routine by making it a habit. I made sure that personal development remained a top priority by setting aside time each day to engage in learning activities. I eventually found a true enthusiasm for lifelong learning and actively sought out opportunities to learn new things.

This mentality change significantly impacted my career and personal development. I improved in my ability to adapt, be resilient, and have confidence when facing new obstacles. My network grew as a result of my continued learning, and I was able to make crucial connections and collaborate on projects.

Most significantly, I found happiness and pleasure in developing a passion for lifelong learning. It gave my journey of personal development a feeling of direction and joy. I learned that growth is a constant, ongoing endeavor by embracing lifelong learning.

The Techniques!

Accept Curiosity and Skepticism

Embracing curiosity and inquisitiveness is the first step in developing a passion for lifelong learning. Be curious about the world and open to discovering novel concepts. Never stop being curious about the world around you; keep asking questions, and looking for solutions.

Set Learning Objectives

Establish clear educational objectives that are in line with your interests and desires. Make a plan to accomplish your goals by identifying knowledge or skill areas you desire to advance. Goals should be broken down into smaller, more manageable steps, and progress should be marked by milestones. For ongoing learning, this process offers motivation and direction.

Adopt a Growth Mindset

Develop a growth mindset, which is the conviction that skills and intelligence can be improved with commitment and effort. Maintain a positive outlook on learning, see failure as a stepping stone to achievement, and embrace obstacles as opportunities for progress. People with a growth mindset are empowered to accept ongoing learning as a natural component of their personal and professional progress.

Diversify the Types of Learning

Investigate many teaching techniques to find the ones that work best for you. Take online courses, attend workshops, participate in debates, read books, listen to podcasts, and look for mentorship. Try out various strategies to see which one appeals to you and keeps you motivated.

Create a Community of Learning

Find a group of learners who are as passionate about lifelong learning as you are. Participate in debates, impart knowledge, and work on projects together. Join learning communities, take part in professional networks, and go to seminars or conferences. Growth can be accelerated and inspiration can be given by the support and pooled knowledge of a learning community.

Establish a Learning Habit

Make studying a part of your everyday schedule by setting aside time for it. Make time each day or week to do learning-related activities. Just like any other important work, learning should be prioritized. Making studying a habit will ensure continual improvement because it will become embedded in your way of life.

Chapter Four

The Development of Financial Intelligence

We attend schools, colleges, and universities in order to finish our education and begin earning a living. To make a living, we choose to work, pursue certain professions, or launch our own enterprises. But which of these organizations equips us to handle our own hard-earned cash? I am quite sure there are few of them.

Financial literacy is the capacity to properly manage our finances by creating systematic budgets, eliminating debt, choosing what to buy and sell, and finally becoming financially independent. Financial literacy is the ability to apply fundamental financial management ideas in daily life.

Everything becomes a part of financial literacy, from straightforward actions like keeping track of our spending and realizing that we must spend money if we like a product to weighing the value of time saved versus money lost, paying our taxes and filing tax returns, concluding property deals, etc.

We are not expected to understand the specifics of financial management as humans. But it's crucial to manage our personal money so that it doesn't negatively impact us and our families. We do not want to find ourselves going through the day without food or money.

Money and Wealth

Our lives are significantly influenced by money and wealth, which affects our possibilities, choices, and general well-being. A comprehensive understanding of wealth and money, however, extends beyond their material components. It entails understanding their underlying significance, committing to ethical financial behavior, and attaining holistic prosperity that goes beyond monetary worth. People can make wise judgments, achieve financial security, and lead satisfying lives by gaining a thorough understanding of wealth and money.

Economic transactions can be facilitated by the use of money as a medium of trade. It has value and enables us to buy products and services. But to comprehend money, one must explore all of its facets. It entails understanding its place in the economy, its various manifestations, and the supply and demand laws that determine its value. Money is a tool that allows us to pursue our objectives and dreams as well as a way to amass material goods.

Contrarily, wealth covers a wider range of ideas that go beyond financial holdings. It encompasses not only material resources but also intangible ones like expertise, relationships, talents, health, and general well-being. Recognizing the various aspects of our lives that money encompasses is essential to understanding it. It involves recognizing the fullness and richness that may be found in experiences, growth, and deep relationships.

Understanding money and wealth requires both financial literacy and responsible money management. Acquiring knowledge and understanding of financial ideas and principles is necessary for financial literacy. Learning the fundamentals of retirement planning, debt management, investing, and budgeting are required. People can acquire the skills they need to make wise financial decisions, avoid financial hazards, and secure their financial future by increasing their financial literacy.

Budgeting, saving, investing, and debt management all go under the umbrella of responsible money management. It entails developing a budget that is in line with your financial priorities and goals, keeping track of your spending, and making sure that your income and spending are in balance. Effective financial planning enables people to deploy funds to meet both short- and long-term objectives while preserving their financial security. It also entails prudent debt management, a grasp of interest rates, and the creation of repayment strategies.

Building money over time depends heavily on investing. Allocating resources to assets with growth potential is part of it. However, learning about investing entails more than just building wealth. Understanding investment concepts like diversification, risk management, and long-term thinking are required. Individuals can make well-informed investing choices that fit their financial objectives and risk tolerance by grasping these ideas.

Although wealth and money are significant, a thorough comprehension of them goes beyond their financial elements. It entails accepting the idea of holistic riches, which includes mental, emotional, and physical well. True riches consist of things like happiness, relationships, personal development, and health. Finding a balance between material gain and general well-being is the goal of holistic wealth. It entails realizing that true riches results from having a sense of fulfillment in life, living in accordance with one's values, and having a sense of purpose.

Mindset and attitude are key components in understanding money and wealth. Changing from a scarcity mentality to an abundance mentality is necessary to have a positive outlook on riches. It entails practicing gratitude for the resources you have right now, emphasizing experiences over things, and coordinating your financial objectives with your moral principles. A positive outlook encourages prudent financial conduct, establishes a positive relationship with money, and empowers people to make choices that result in long-term financial security.

Furthermore, comprehending money and wealth requires taking into account how they affect society and the environment. Having money can help you influence the world for the better and improve other people's lives. Wealthy people appreciate the value of social responsibility and use their money to promote issues they are passionate about. They work hard to have a beneficial effect on society and leave a lasting legacy.

Making a Strategic Financial Plan

Have you ever considered what your life may be like if you had the option of working or not?

What would life be like if you had the freedom to leave your job or business whenever you wanted? You've probably given this concept some thought, even if you currently enjoy your work or have your ideal career. "Yes, I enjoy my work. However, what if I didn't have to?"

A level of financial security that many individuals strive for but few really attain is necessary for making work a choice. Why? Due to the fact that they never learned how to make money. They may be able to work hard and earn a substantial salary, but they lack the skills to make money work for them.

How to Develop a Wealth Plan

Evaluating One's Present Financial Situation

Making an assessment of your present financial condition is the first step in creating a strategic wealth plan. This entails determining your overall net worth as well as your assets, liabilities, income, and spending. You can find your financial landscape's advantages, disadvantages, and opportunities for growth by studying it.

Having Specific Financial Goals

An integral part of a strategic wealth plan is setting clear and specific financial goals. You can successfully prioritize your efforts and distribute resources when you have goals because they provide you direction and purpose. Declaring your goals clearly will help direct your financial decisions and actions, whether they be to buy a home, pay for college, or enjoy a happy retirement.

Budgeting and Cash Flow Management

A strategic wealth plan comprises setting up a budget and efficiently handling cash flow. You can allocate money from a budget to debt repayment, savings, investments, and necessary expenses. It enables you to keep tabs on your expenditure, find places where you can make savings, and make sure you are residing within your means. By optimizing and coordinating your financial resources with your objectives, effective cash flow management makes this possible.

Taking Care of Debt and Developing Credit

A strategic wealth plan includes credit development and debt control. It includes figuring out which debts to pay off first, setting up a repayment plan, and reducing high-interest debt. Reducing the burden of interest payments and improving your creditworthiness through responsible debt management enables you to establish a strong financial base.

Setting-up a Fund for Unforeseen

An essential element of a strategic wealth plan is an emergency fund. It serves as a safety net for money, acting as a cushion in the event of unforeseen costs or interruptions in income. Having an emergency fund gives you peace of mind, protects your assets, and decreases the need for borrowing during a crisis.

Putting Investment Strategies in Practice

Investment tactics are essential for building and expanding wealth. In order to create an investment plan that meets your needs, a strategic wealth plan takes into account your risk tolerance, time horizon, and financial goals. This may entail diversifying your holdings, taking into account various asset classes, and, if necessary, consulting a specialist.

Managing Risk and Protecting Asset

Risk management and asset protection are addressed in a complete wealth plan. To ensure that you are adequately protected for yourself and your assets, this includes assessing insurance coverage including life, health, disability, and property insurance. Identifying and reducing risks will protect your assets and ensure your family's financial stability.

Building a Legacy and Estate Planning

Regardless of your net worth, estate planning is a crucial component of a strategic wealth plan. In order to make sure that your assets are dispersed in accordance with your preferences, it entails drafting a will, setting up trusts, and choosing beneficiaries. You can also reduce your tax obligations and safeguard your money for future generations by using estate planning.

Developing Your Investing Art

The world of investing can be thrilling and intimidating, full of chances, and dangers. It necessitates a thorough comprehension of financial markets, the capacity to evaluate investment possibilities, and the will to make wise choices. Let me describe the process I went through to learn the art of investing and how it affected my financial destiny.

I think this should boost and energize your interest. I had little expertise and less information as I started down the investing path. My motivation came from a desire to increase my fortune and safeguard my financial future. But I soon discovered that more than just a desire for financial gain was necessary for effective investing. It required a dedication to learning, methodical decision-making, and a long-term outlook.

Getting Investment Information

I immersed myself in learning about investing to build a strong foundation. I read voraciously, went to seminars, and consulted with seasoned investors for guidance. I became knowledgeable about important investing concepts like risk and return, asset allocation, and valuation techniques. I gained knowledge about how to interpret financial statements, evaluate market trends, and comprehend the elements that affect the success of investments.

Goal-setting for Investment

A vital stage in my path became establishing specific investment goals. Whether it was capital growth, providing passive income, or supporting long-term financial goals, I clearly stated my objectives. I was able to evaluate the viability of various investment options by establishing clear, quantifiable goals that gave my investing plan direction.

Creating an Investment Plan

I made a unique investing plan with my objectives in mind. I understood the value of diversification in reducing risk and maximizing rewards. To create a portfolio that was well-balanced, I distributed my investments among various asset classes, including stocks, bonds, real estate, and mutual funds. In addition, I created an investing schedule that took both my short- and long-term investment horizons into account.

Adopting a Long-term Viewpoint

I learned the benefits of a long-term perspective by mastering the art of investing. I was aware that noise and short-term market swings can detract from the main objective of wealth growth. I could weather market turbulence and benefit from compounding over time by concentrating on the long-term potential of my investments.

Understanding Mistakes

I ran through investing difficulties and made blunders along the way. But rather than seeing these situations as failures, I saw them as wonderful lessons. I took the time to consider my choices, examine the causes of any defeats, and modify my tactics as necessary. I was able to improve my investing strategy and grow as a more competent and resilient investor by taking lessons from my blunders.

Looking for Expert Advice

Recognizing the complexities of the investment environment, I occasionally consulted a specialist. I recognized the benefits of working with financial advisors who were knowledgeable in particular fields, such as tax preparation, retirement planning, or estate planning. I was able to make more intelligent judgments by working with experts to better understand the complexities of investing.

Accepting Emotional Self-Control

Emotional self-control is necessary to master the art of investing. When dealing with the uncertainties and vagaries of the market, emotions inevitably come into play. I did, however, learn to keep my emotions out of my financial selections and refrain from making snap judgments driven by either greed or fear. I established a rigorous approach and stuck to my investment plan despite the turbulence.

Celebrating Achievements While Being Humble

I enjoyed the wins along the way as I continued on my financial path. Recognizing these accomplishments — whether it was hitting a financial milestone or beating market expectations — boosted my self-assurance and drive. At the same time, I maintained my humility, realizing that learning about investment is a never-ending process and there is always more to learn.

Chapter Five

The Influence of Connections

The capacity of networking to influence both our personal and professional life is enormous. It is a purposeful and intentional strategy that can open up innumerable opportunities, promote personal development, and build a network of support. It goes beyond simply mingling or exchanging business cards. People can connect with like-minded professionals, mentors, collaborators, and new clients through networking, which will ultimately help them succeed.

Building relationships is at the heart of networking. It entails actively interacting with people in your sector or field, taking part in activities, joining online communities, and looking for networking possibilities. People that put in the time and effort to network can profit in a variety of ways that can change their lives.

The increase in opportunity is one of networking's major advantages. People can access a multitude of information, perceptions, and resources by networking. They have access to data on open positions, market trends, and potential collaborations that may not be easily accessible through other means. Opportunities frequently come about as a result of introductions, recommendations, and referrals made inside a strong network.

Networking enables people to create lasting connections. It involves creating true ties based on trust, shared values, and mutual objectives, which go beyond surface interactions. By making an investment in these connections, people can build a network of experts who are prepared to offer direction, counsel, and support when required. In-depth connections made through networking can result in partnerships, mentorship opportunities, and even lifetime friendships.

Networking serves as a forum for learning and sharing information. The sharing of ideas, insights, and best practices is made possible by conversing with people from various backgrounds and industries. Individuals can stay current on the newest trends, developments, and opportunities in their fields by taking part in industry events, conferences, and online networks. Through ongoing learning, networking cultivates a favorable environment for both personal and professional development.

Networking improves visibility and self-branding. Individuals can demonstrate their knowledge, abilities, and distinctive value offer by actively participating in networking events, speaking engagements, and online forums. One's professional reputation can be improved by contributing to discussions, sharing insights, and exhibiting thought leadership within a network. People can leave a lasting impression and stand out from the crowd by networking.

Additionally, networking can lead to mentorship and direction. You may acquire priceless insights and counsel by getting in touch with seasoned experts in your sector. Mentors can offer advice on overcoming obstacles, share their own experiences, and offer support during difficult job transitions. A mentor's expertise and advice can hasten one's professional and personal development while assisting one in avoiding typical mistakes.

By forming connections, you can build a network that gives you confidence and emotional support. Finding like-minded colleagues with comparable objectives and aims can motivate you and give you a sense of community. Networking groups frequently provide a secure environment where members may discuss problems, celebrate victories, and get guidance. A robust network's ability to provide emotional support can increase one's resilience, self-assurance, and general well-being.

Last but not least, networking is about more than just receiving; it's also about giving and paying it forward. People help others in their network grow and succeed by imparting knowledge, providing support, and setting up meetings. Within the networking community, establishing mutually beneficial connections and assisting others in their activities helps to promote a culture of cooperation and giving.

5 Pros of Networking for Entrepreneurs

Access to Opportunities: By introducing you to possible customers, partners, investors, and mentors, networking helps you increase your opportunities.

Knowledge and Insights: Networking gives you access to useful information, industry trends, and insights that can help you remain on top of things.

Relationship Building: Through networking, you can create solid, win-win connections that may result in partnerships and collaborations.

Support Network: Through networking, you can find others who share your interests and goals and who can help you by understanding your obstacles.

Greater Visibility: By actively networking, you can become more visible in your field, which can increase your chances of success.

5 Cons of Networking for Entrepreneurs

Time and Effort: Attending events, interacting with others, and maintaining connections all take time and effort.

Networking gatherings can be intimidating and anxiety-inducing for introverted people.

Lack of Sincerity: Some networking encounters may come out as transactional and devoid of real connection.

Competition: In businesses with intense competition, networking may become cutthroat, and standing out can be difficult.

Unpredictable Returns: Not all networking activities produce returns right once, and it could take some time before you start to reap the rewards.

Effective Relationship Building and Communication

Relationship Foundation

All business partnerships are built on effective communication. These connections are built on how we communicate with one another both inside and outside of our organization. You can develop the required interpersonal connections to launch your firm if you can properly convey your ideas.

Talk with the Staff

Internal communication should be the starting point. Your workers will feel interested and driven if you can effectively explain your ideas to them. It enables people to work together, invent, and create new goods, strengthening and advancing your company. Additionally, it's crucial to make sure your team can communicate well because you never know who among your employees might have the bright idea that will propel your business to new heights. It will show in their job and improve their relationship with your clients if your team members feel valued and comfortable approaching you.

Engage Customers

Your customers and future customers are the target audience for your next crucial communication. Customers can learn more about you and your services while also receiving information about your goods and services if you communicate with them successfully. When it comes to your consumer base, your relationship is a two-way street; if you pay attention to their demands, it will help you add a personal touch, develop a relationship, and win them over.

Customer loyalty is essential to a firm, especially in the early stages. The best form of advertising you can use is a devoted customer who will not only bring you to repeat business but also recommend you to their friends and family.

You may adjust your marketing to draw in more customers by knowing the best ways to communicate with your customers. You only get one chance to make a first impression on a potential consumer since opinions are formed rapidly. Therefore, it is crucial that you leave a positive impression and convey your main points.

Finally, have you thought about how you interact with various third parties, such as possible partners and investors? It may assist them comprehend your mission and ethos.

Again, this is not a one-way street; if you are communicating well, you will also get feedback from outside ideas and proposals. You never know what suggestions they might provide or how taking their advice might alter your company.

Role Models and Mentors

Mentors and role models encourage people to live a specific way and have an impact on the crucial choices they make in life. Although the phrases "role models" and "mentors" are frequently used interchangeably, they have clear distinctions. The explicit definition of a mentor is a person with more experience and expertise who, typically known to the other person, directs and instructs them in person. On the other hand, a role model is typically someone who is unknown to the person but who they look up to and who has an impact on their behavior.

In conclusion, a mentor shows you how to develop into the best version of yourself, whereas a role model is someone you strive to be like. A person can be both a mentor and a role model since these two concepts can be combined both generally and in the world of business.

We can decide how to combine the two within a corporation when we can identify the fundamental distinctions.

Anyone can serve as a mentor, but not everyone can serve as a role model. Mentoring has great power. A person can become a better person through mentoring, and their talents and abilities can grow as well. So begin by developing a strong mentor-mentee relationship in order to become the best mentor possible. You can and will become your mentee's role model by being a good mentor.

Chapter Six

Overcoming Challenges and Rebounding

I started a business because I thought it had a lot of potential. I invested everything I had—my heart, my soul, and my money—into it, thinking that success was only around the corner. The reality, however, had other ideas. The company encountered unforeseen difficulties, such as changes in the market, financial limitations, and fierce rivalry. The setback was heartbreaking, and I started to doubt my skills, my judgment, and my future in business.

I at first felt overwhelmed and defeated. The obstacle appeared insurmountable, and I was inclined to give up on my goals entirely. I was aware, though, that giving in to hopelessness was not an option. I had to muster the fortitude to overcome the setback, draw lessons from the event, and pave a fresh course for the future.

Recognizing my feelings was the first step in recovering from the setback. I gave myself permission to experience the disappointment, annoyance, and melancholy that came with the failure. I understood that obstacles are a normal part of any trip, and it was crucial to work through these feelings before continuing. I confided in dependable friends and mentors who offered a sympathetic ear and priceless counsel.

I then decided to adopt a growth mentality instead of obsessing over my failure. I reframed the setback as a chance for knowledge gain and personal development. I saw it as an opportunity to learn important lessons, hone my abilities, and build resilience rather than as a reflection of my ability. I adopted the viewpoint that failures serve as stepping stones to success and that, with tenacity and a can-do attitude, I could overcome any obstacle.

I went through a process of introspection and analysis, looking at the elements that contributed to the failure. I recognized some areas where I could do better, such as market research, financial preparation, and flexibility in response to changing conditions. I searched for information from specialists, went to conferences and workshops, and immersed myself in learning opportunities to build the abilities required for success in the future.

I also surrounded myself with a strong network of friends and family. I sought advice from mentors who had overcome adversity and come out stronger. Their advice and inspiration were vital in rekindling my resolve and assisting me in viewing the setback as a brief detour rather than a long-term obstacle. They gave me confidence and inspired me to keep going in spite of the difficulties because they believed in me.

I took calculated risks and adopted a philosophy of constant development as I moved forward. I understood that failures are chances for growth and innovation rather than signs of failure. In order to achieve a competitive edge, I improved my business strategies, investigated new markets, and used technology. I developed my ability to embrace uncertainty and adjust to shifting conditions with each step.

Over time, I came to understand that failures are simply a chapter on the path to success rather than the end of the road. The setback I experienced evolved into a formative event that molded my personality, boosted my resilience, and motivated my tenacity. It helped me understand the value of tenacity, flexibility, and confidence.

Everyone has setbacks at some point in their lives. Dealing with failures in a healthy way is crucial for entrepreneurs because they are a necessary part of the road to success. Never forget that you can quickly recover from failure and get back on track. An entrepreneur's success is determined by what he learned from his failures, not how many times he failed in his career.

However, it is how we handle these difficulties and obstacles that establish our character and directs our course for the future.

Resilience and the Art of Bouncing Back

The route of life is full of unexpected turns and detours. We face a variety of challenges along the way that put our fortitude, tenacity, and ability to overcome adversity to the test. The skill of overcoming these obstacles while remaining strong and intelligent is known as resilience. It is the capacity to adjust to, learn from, and develop from hardship while utilizing adversity's transforming power to advance. In this part, we will examine the idea of resilience, its importance in our lives, and methods for developing and enhancing this crucial quality.

Resilience is the capability to face adversity head-on, overcome hurdles, and prosper in the face of challenges rather than just the absence of difficulty or the capacity to avoid difficulties. Resilience on the emotional, psychological, and cognitive levels is a dynamic, multifaceted trait. People who are resilient have a specific set of abilities, attitudes, and viewpoints that help them bounce back from setbacks, keep a positive attitude, and adjust to changing situations.

In both our personal and professional lives, resilience is crucial. It gives us the tools we need to negotiate life's uncertainties and complexities, empowering us to overcome setbacks, deal with stress, and persevere in the pursuit of our objectives. Building deeper connections, retaining our emotional health, and approaching problems with confidence and self-belief are all made possible by resilience. In essence, resilience gives us the ability to turn challenges into opportunities and setbacks into stepping stones for development and achievement.

Adopting a growth mindset, or the conviction that one's skills and intelligence can be improved through hard work, education, and perseverance, is necessary for developing resilience. By adopting this perspective, we can see obstacles as chances for development rather than insurmountable obstacles. We may utilize the force of resilience to adapt, advance, and get better by concentrating on the lessons discovered through mistakes and setbacks.

Effective emotion comprehension and management are necessary for resilience. Being emotionally aware enables us to recognize our emotions even in the face of hardship. We can develop emotional resilience, which gives us the inner strength and stability to face challenges and make wise decisions, by acknowledging and processing our feelings.

The encouragement of a powerful and supportive network is essential for developing resilience. We can improve our capacity to recover from setbacks by surrounding ourselves with people who support us, encourage us, and lend a sympathetic ear. Our resilience can be greatly increased and useful perspectives and insights can be gained by talking about our experiences, asking for help, and receiving support from dependable friends, family, or mentors.

Building resilience and growing self-compassion require taking care of oneself, taking part in enjoyable activities, and accepting a good self-image. A belief in our capacity to learn, adapt, and grow serves as the fuel for resilience. We transfer our attention from the constraints of the present to the opportunities of the future by keeping a growth-oriented attitude. We may enhance our resilience by accepting obstacles as chances for growth, innovation, and self-improvement by adopting this mindset.

Failure into Opportunities

Life will inevitably include failure. It is the sour aftertaste of disappointment, the burning sensation of unfulfilled expectations, and the sense of failing. Failure need not be the end of the path, though. Instead, it can act as a springboard for opportunity and growth. Failure can become a stepping stone to achievement if we shift our attitude and adopt a resilient mindset. Let's look at how to harness the transforming power of failure and how to turn setbacks into opportunities.

Failure is a normal aspect of learning; it does not indicate our merit or competence. We have an option when we fail: to wallow in self-doubt and despair or to see it as a worthwhile lesson and a chance for development. We can achieve both personal and professional growth by embracing the latter.

Transforming our fixed perspective into a growth mindset is one of the first stages in converting failure into an opportunity. Failure is seen as a sign of incapacity or a fundamental defect by those with fixed mindsets. A growth mentality, on the other hand, views failure as an opportunity to grow, learn, and advance. It understands that failure is merely a momentary setback on the road to success rather than a permanent state. We may develop resilience, accept challenges, and take the chances presented by failures by adopting a growth mindset.

Adopting a process of self-reflection and analysis is a crucial component in transforming failure into chances. Failure can be a chance for us to gather insightful knowledge and learn from our mistakes rather than obsessing over its negative elements. We can find opportunities for development and create plans for future success by examining ourselves with questions like "What went wrong?" and "What could I have done differently?" Failure gives us a fresh perspective and an opportunity to reevaluate our objectives, strategies, and top priorities.

Humility and a readiness to accept responsibility for our errors are necessary for learning from failure. It's crucial to refrain from blaming others or outside forces for our mistakes. Instead, we must accept responsibility for our acts and acknowledge our part in the outcome. This gives us the ability to grow from our mistakes and make the necessary changes to prevent doing them again.

Additionally, failure provides a chance to develop resilience. When we experience failures, we have the opportunity to hone our capacity to recover and persevere in the face of difficulty. Our ability to remain upbeat, persevere through difficulties, and adjust to shifting circumstances is known as resilience. By strengthening our resilience, we improve our ability to deal with setbacks in the future and turn them into learning experiences.

Taking calculated chances and moving outside of our comfort zones are frequently necessary to turn failure into possibilities. It necessitates accepting uncertainty and being receptive to novel possibilities. Failure can spur creativity and innovation by encouraging us to consider different avenues and strategies. We can overcome our fear of failure and expand our horizons of possibility by accepting failure as a necessary component of the trip.

Finally, it's critical to ask for help and direction from others after you've failed. Having a network of friends, family, mentors, and coworkers at our sides can offer us support, guidance, and insightful advice. They can discuss their own failures and offer new viewpoints as well as advice on how to deal with difficulties. Our capacity to transform setbacks into opportunities can tremendously benefit from the insight and encouragement of others.

Chapter Seven

The Millionaire Mindset in Action

Success is a long story, indeed!

Everyone wants to be prosperous. We all want to live comfortably, with a large, attractive house, a decent automobile, a sizable bank account, etc. You must engage in a ferocious battle if you want to succeed.

Nothing succeeds that hasn't been analyzed and thought through, according to the science of success. The strongest guys in this world conquer by using their expertise.

The one factor that can ensure your success in your pursuit of achievement is your level of knowledge. The most useful instrument you need to arm yourself with in order to succeed is more good knowledge.

Let's devour books and learn a ton of useful information.

What is a success or being successful?

Many individuals mistake the meaning of the word "success." Real success is achieved. It is a person or object that has succeeded by reaching a "good result by acceptable means" or the act of accomplishing something you had been planning to do or obtain.

Stress the phrase "good result by acceptable means," which is the only standard by which success is judged.

Yes, success is only defined as a positive outcome. Success or a good outcome indicates that the proper approach was used. For an outcome to be deemed good, it "must" be the product of proper execution.

In most cases, becoming millionaires is unlikely.

In all honesty, most people lack the necessary skills to become millionaires.

This is why:

1. **Lack of a clear goal**

The vast majority of people lack a clear purpose in life. This indicates that the majority of people are unaware of their true purpose for existing or what they hope to achieve during their time on Earth.

Not HOW TO BECOME A MILLIONAIRE but WHY YOU SHOULD BECOME A MILLIONAIRE is the most crucial query.

Many millionaires didn't simply become wealthy by pursuing their own narcissistic desires to own expensive homes and cars. To improve the lives of their families and communities, they had more overarching objectives and goals.

2. **Lack of perfect strategies**

Many people are unaware that bad plans never work. Only flawless plans are successful. Millionaires understand how to create flawless plans by outlining them in detail. They achieve their specific goals by meticulously adhering to the plan.

3. **Lacking a strong desire**

Since burning desire is the fuel that powers purpose, it follows that if you don't have one, you'll also lack blazing desire.

As a result, the vast majority of people in the world who lack a clear purpose and a strong drive for success are unable to develop both inside and externally as human beings.

Numerous world conquerors, like Napoleon, Nelson Mandela, Julius Caesar, and Alexander the Great, all possessed intense, burning drives. The same applies to those who excelled as sportsmen, boxing champions, or millionaires.

4. **Procrastination**

Failure to take action is what is meant by procrastination. The biggest obstacle to becoming a millionaire and the biggest enemy of success is procrastination.

Most people simply float through life and live without any clear goal or direction. They pass a lot of time thinking, drooling, and doing nothing. They consequently end up getting impoverished.

5. Discipline issues

Perhaps one of the biggest obstacles to financial success is a lack of discipline. There are many unsuccessful people in the world who simply lacked financial restraint and sound strategy.

No such thing as an accident exists. Each failure is the outcome of a mistake in human judgment. Everyone receives opportunities and chances, but not all at once, and when they do, a lack of vision, a lack of financial restraint, and a lack of readiness seriously impair one's ability to succeed financially.

6. Lack of endurance

The majority of people simply lack the patience necessary to become millionaires. Think about when you sow a seed; you probably have no idea how it will sprout a few days or weeks later. Additionally, monitoring the development daily is not helpful.

However, when you inspect it a few weeks later, you'll notice that the buds have proliferated and the plant is starting to grow. After a few more weeks, it grows into a large plant. All of them need effort, waiting, and a process. Here patience becomes important.

Work is the time and effort you put into anything, whereas seed is the basic material you put into the soil. The process is what operates without your intervention. You have no power over it.

The majority of individuals would probably prefer to sow a seed and then harvest its fruit the next morning.

7.   **Focus deficit**

According to Bruce Lee, a legend in the Kung Fu martial arts, the effective warrior is the everyday guy with laser-like focus.

Lack of focus is, as we all know, the biggest barrier to financial success. The majority of millionaires I know have a laser-like focus.

Jack Ma, a Chinese billionaire, and the former executive chairman and co-founder of the Alibaba Group, frequently claims to have 5,000 new company ideas every day. Unfortunately, he must decline them all in favor of staying committed to providing top-notch service to the millions of clients and suppliers that visit his online stores every day.

8.   **Work diligently and judiciously**

Because they never learned how to work wisely, the majority of individuals will never become millionaires. You may have heard that perseverance pays rewards. Indeed. I believe that working hard on its own can never be fruitful; you must also work smart.

Getting affluent in the 19th century took around 30 years. In the 20th century, getting affluent took fewer than 20 years. In the 21st century, with a clear and perfect plan, being wealthy could take as little as six months.

All of these hinge on the clever use of a straightforward law known as leverage.

Millionaires are skilled at maximizing the time of others.

Millionaires are skilled at using other people's funds as leverage.

Millionaires are adept at utilizing the abilities and skills of others.

Millionaires acquire skills in utilizing automation and machines.

9.   **Lack of life-long learning – constantly reading books**

Most people stop studying after they matriculate, graduate from high school, or enter the workforce. Although it's a way of life, most people will never learn anything new that will help them improve their lives.

An example would be the factory-installed default settings of a computer. We hardly ever use a computer without first personalizing it with our own preferences and settings, which typically entails installing specialized software.

Although we rarely acknowledge it, humans and computers share many similarities. As a result, the majority of people never discover new techniques for enhancing their way of life and financial security.

10. Absence of coherence

Most people lack consistency, which prevents them from becoming millionaires.

The majority of millionaires and billionaires I know put one single business concept or product into action and stuck with it for a very long time.

Unbelievably, Coca-Cola is among the brands with the best consistency worldwide. The general concepts in its well-known advertising campaigns, which frequently alter, remain constant. Coca-Cola is renowned for promoting the concepts of joy, community, and refreshment in its advertisements around the world.

This technique has been very successful over the course of its 132-year history, bringing in a sizable profit for its investors. How many businesses are around that long?

Stories of Entrepreneurial Success

Entrepreneurship is a challenging, risky, and uncertain endeavor. However, it is a road that can also result in extraordinary achievement and fulfillment. Numerous businesspeople have overcome obstacles throughout history to achieve their goals, change the world, and leave a lasting legacy. Before we wrap things up, let's take a quick look at a few successful business stories from diverse industries, examining their journeys, the lessons they may impart, and the motivation they can offer.

Apple Inc. – Steve Jobs:

Steve Jobs, the co-founder of Apple Inc., has one of the most well-known success tales in the field of entrepreneurship. Jobs' career was full of ups and downs, but his unwavering love for creativity and design inspired him to change the face of technology. Jobs transformed numerous sectors and became a symbol of invention and tenacity. He started the first Apple computer in the garage of his parents and later released ground-breaking goods like the iPhone and iPad.

The most important things we need to take note of from Steve Jobs' success are the value of following your passion, thinking beyond the box, and persevering in the face of challenges. Jobs overcame obstacles and revolutionized how we engage with technology because of his unyielding faith in his vision and unrelenting pursuit of greatness.

OWN Network – Oprah Winfrey:

The life of Oprah Winfrey is a tribute to the strength of resiliency, tenacity, and purposeful living. She was born into poverty and struggled with many obstacles throughout her life. Winfrey did, however, succeed in creating an empire via her tenacity and unbreakable character.

Winfrey rose to prominence in media and philanthropy by hosting The Oprah Winfrey Show, founding her own media firm, Harpo Productions, and establishing the OWN Network.

We may learn from Winfrey's success how to embrace authenticity, play to one's abilities, and have a beneficial impact on the world. She persevered in the face of difficulty by remaining true to herself, engaging her audience deeply, and using her platform to raise awareness of significant causes. Winfrey's path is a prime example of the transforming power of using one's own experience to inspire and empower others.

SpaceX, Tesla, and more – Elon Musk:

Elon Musk has demonstrated audacity, ambition, and dogged pursuit of disruptive innovation throughout his professional career. Tesla, SpaceX, Neuralink, and The Boring Company are just a few of the ground-breaking businesses that Musk co-founded. He has advanced technology through his endeavors, transformed the market for electric vehicles, and led the charge to investigate space colonization.

We may learn from Musk's success how important it is to be brave, take calculated risks, and question the status quo. Even in the face of resistance and challenges, he is renowned for his unrelenting dedication to his mission. Numerous businesspeople have been motivated to think large, push limits, and foresee an innovative future by Musk's unrelenting pursuit of innovations.

Spanx – Sara Blakely:

The success of Sara Blakely is proof of the value of tenacity, fortitude, and the capacity to spot and seize chances. Blakely is the creator of the billion-dollar shapewear company called Spanx. Multiple rejections and losses accompanied her path to success, but she never wavered in her commitment to her idea and her capacity to change and grow.

Blakely's success story demonstrates the value of accepting failure as a teaching opportunity, welcoming innovation, and having faith in one's gut. She demonstrated the power of entrepreneurship and the influence that one idea can have by spotting a market gap and creating a solution that addressed a common pain point.

Leaving a Viable Legacy

We all have a profound desire to make a difference in the world and be remembered for something significant even after we are gone. Making a difference, advancing society, and leaving a lasting legacy all include making a beneficial impact on future generations. It reflects our moral principles, worldview, and the legacy we want to leave behind.

Beyond tangible wealth or achievements, legacy refers to the influence we have on people's lives and the good we do for the world. It involves leaving a legacy that motivates and inspires others to carry on the task we started. Legacy can be demonstrated in a variety of ways, including through interpersonal connections, professional success, philanthropy, and creative activities. Each person has the ability to create a lasting legacy that is distinctive and important.

Choosing your principles and establishing your mission is the first step towards leaving a lasting legacy. What do you believe in? What tenets govern your life? You can discover the core of who you are and the influence you wish to have by thinking about these questions. Your legacy reflects your principles, worldview, and the impression you want to make on the world. You can make sure that your legacy captures the essence of who you are and the influence you want to have by ensuring that your actions and decisions are in line with your beliefs and purpose.

Personal connections are one of the most powerful methods to leave a lasting impression. The relationships we build with our loved ones, friends, and communities can have an effect that lasts for many generations. We foster a good shift in these relationships by giving them our time, love, and support. Our deeds, words, and presence can uplift and empower others, influencing their course in life and fostering their personal development. By fostering deep and meaningful connections, we transmit the principles and knowledge that will go on long after we are gone.

A lasting legacy is also greatly influenced by professional accomplishments. Through our job, we have the chance to influence industries, inspire future generations, and make a difference in our specialized sectors. We improve society by breaking down barriers, achieving excellence, and having a positive impact in the field we choose. Our efforts can have a lasting impact that affects upcoming generations of professionals by influencing how people think, work, and create.

Yet another way to leave a lasting impact is through philanthropy. Giving back to causes and groups that share our ideals helps to bring about constructive social change. Philanthropy enables us to have a real and long-lasting impact on the lives of others, whether it is through monetary contributions, volunteer work, or supporting social causes. We may affect positive change that lasts much beyond our lifetimes by contributing to causes we are passionate about.

Another avenue for leaving a lasting impact is through creative pursuits. The ability to inspire future generations lies in the creative expressions of art, music, and literature. We can affect people's hearts and minds, elicit emotions, shift viewpoints, and spark change through our creative efforts. Our artistic activities have the power to change the world, whether we're writing a book, producing a work of art, or performing music.

It is essential to act with intention, purpose, and authenticity if you want to leave a lasting legacy. Consciously make decisions that are in line with your principles, and constantly do things that advance society and the well-being of others. Accept opportunities for development and learning, as they help you grow personally and professionally and leave a lasting legacy. Always keep in mind that leaving a lasting legacy is not about pursuing popularity or glory, but rather about making a meaningful contribution to society and inspiring the next generation.

Conclusion

For those looking for success and wealth in both their personal and professional life, "The Millionaire Mindset: How to Overcome Hurdles and Succeed in Business" is a complete handbook. This book has given helpful tips, tricks, and guidelines for developing the attitude required to achieve one's objectives.

The millionaire mindset comprises a holistic way of living rather than being restricted to material wealth. It entails adopting a growth mentality, viewing difficulties as chances for improvement, and persevering in the face of setbacks. It places a strong emphasis on the value of positive attitude cultivation, visualization, and belief.

We have covered a wide range of subjects in this book, including time management, financial literacy, investment, networking, and effective communication. We now understand the value of having specific objectives, developing a vision, and taking calculated risks. We have also emphasized the importance of resiliency, recovering from failure, and accepting failure as a stepping stone to achievement.

In our quest for success, the importance of mentors and role models has been underlined since they offer direction, motivation, and support.

Readers can develop the attitude and abilities required to successfully negotiate the difficulties of business and reach their desired level of success by putting the principles and tactics presented in this book into practice. Although there will likely be ups and downs along the way, people may overcome obstacles and build a life that is abundant and fulfilling by exercising patience, self-control, and a growth-oriented viewpoint.

The millionaire mindset is not something that can be attained fast, and it is crucial for readers to keep this in mind. Consistent effort, learning, and adaptation are required. However, armed with the information and direction provided in this book, readers can boldly set out on their path to success, outfitted with the skills necessary to surmount challenges and capture opportunities.